CW01270213

EAGLE EYE

A KIDS GUIDE TO THE BALD EAGLE

BRIAN THOMAS

BOOKSTEM

Copyright © 2025 by Brian Thomas

All rights reserved.

No part of this book may be reproduced in any form or by any electronic or mechanical means, including information storage and retrieval systems, without written permission from the author, except for the use of brief quotations in a book review.

CONTENTS

1. MEET THE BALD EAGLE — 5
   Why is it called a "bald" eagle? — 11
   Fun facts about bald eagles — 13

2. THE SYMBOL OF A NATION — 19
   The Great Seal of the United States — 22
   Other animals that were considered — 25

3. THE BALD EAGLE IN NATIVE AMERICAN CULTURE — 31
   How feathers were used in ceremonies and traditions — 34
   Stories and myths about the bald eagle — 37

4. BALD EAGLES IN THE WILD — 39
   What they eat and how they hunt — 42
   The role of bald eagles in the ecosystem — 45

5. ALMOST GONE — 49
   The impact of pollution, hunting, and habitat destruction — 52
   How DDT nearly wiped them out — 56

6. SAVING THE BALD EAGLE — 61
   How scientists and conservationists helped — 64
   Bald eagles today — 67

7. BALD EAGLES AND AMERICAN
   PRIDE   71
   How bald eagles are still used as
   symbols   74
   What kids can do to help protect bald
   eagles and other wildlife   76

8. AMAZING BALD EAGLE FACTS   79
   Bald eagle superpowers   82
   Fun trivia   85

1

MEET THE BALD EAGLE

The bald eagle is one of the most recognizable birds in North America. With its sharp beak, powerful wings, and piercing yellow eyes, it looks like it's always paying close attention to what's happening around it. This bird isn't small either. It has an enormous wingspan—sometimes stretching up to seven feet across! That's longer than most kids are tall. When it spreads its wings and soars through the sky, it barely even flaps. Instead, it rides the wind, gliding smoothly over forests, lakes, and rivers.

One of the most striking features of the bald eagle is its coloring. Its dark brown body stands in sharp contrast to its bright white head and tail.

Those white feathers don't show up right away, though. Young bald eagles look completely different from adults. They are mostly brown with white speckles, and it takes about five years for them to develop their famous white heads. Until then, they could easily be mistaken for a different type of eagle.

Despite its name, the bald eagle isn't actually bald. The word "bald" in this case comes from an old English word, **"piebald,"** which means "white-headed." Early English-speaking settlers in North America saw these impressive birds and called them bald eagles, and the name stuck.

Where Bald Eagles Live

Bald eagles are found only in North America. They live in Canada, the United States, and parts of Mexico. Unlike some birds that prefer one type of environment, bald eagles are pretty adaptable. However, there is one thing they always need nearby—water. Rivers, lakes, and coastal areas are perfect homes for bald eagles because they provide plenty of food.

Alaska has the largest population of bald eagles in the world. The cold, rugged landscape might seem like a tough place to live, but for bald eagles, it's perfect. The state has wide-open spaces, towering trees for nesting, and an abundance of fish. In some areas of Alaska, it's not unusual to see dozens of bald eagles in one place. They gather in large numbers, especially near rivers where salmon are plentiful.

Bald eagles also live in the lower 48 states, but they are more common in places with lots of lakes and forests. States like Minnesota, Wisconsin, and Michigan have large bald eagle populations because of their many lakes. The Pacific Northwest, from Washington to Northern California, is another favorite spot. Florida, with its warm climate and wetlands, is home to many bald eagles as well.

Even though they prefer natural environments, bald eagles have been spotted in some surprising places. They can sometimes be seen soaring over big cities, flying near tall buildings or bridges. As long as there's a food source nearby, bald eagles can make a home almost anywhere.

What Bald Eagles Eat

Bald eagles are carnivores, which means they eat meat. Their favorite food is fish. That's why they stick close to lakes and rivers. With their sharp eyesight, they can spot a fish from high up in the air. When they see one swimming near the surface, they dive down, extend their massive talons, and snatch it right out of the water. Their strong grip keeps the fish from slipping away.

While fish is their preferred meal, bald eagles aren't picky eaters. They'll also hunt small mammals like rabbits and squirrels. If they find an easy meal, such as a dead animal, they won't turn it down. They are opportunistic feeders, meaning they take advantage of whatever food is available. Sometimes, they even steal food from other birds, especially ospreys. If an osprey catches a fish, a bald eagle might chase it down, forcing the smaller bird to drop its catch. The eagle then swoops in and takes the fish for itself.

Even though bald eagles are powerful hunters, they don't always succeed. Sometimes, they'll miss a fish or struggle to pull one out of the water if it's too heavy. But their hunting skills, combined with their ability to scavenge, make them one of the top predators in their environment.

Bald Eagle Nests

Bald eagles don't just build nests; they build **huge** nests. Some of the largest bird nests in the world belong to bald eagles. They usually build them high up in trees, often choosing the tallest tree in the area. The higher the nest, the safer it is from predators.

These nests are made out of sticks, but they aren't flimsy. Bald eagles carefully arrange the sticks and use moss, grass, and feathers to make them more comfortable. The nests start off large but get even bigger over time. That's because bald eagles reuse their nests year after year, adding new materials each time they return. Some nests grow so big that they weigh over a ton! One of the largest recorded bald eagle nests measured **9 feet wide and 20 feet deep**—big enough for a person to lie down inside.

Both the male and female bald eagle help build the nest. Once it's finished, the female lays one to three eggs, and both parents take turns keeping them warm. After about 35 days, the eggs hatch, and small, fluffy eaglets emerge. At first, they are completely helpless. They rely on their parents for food and protection. It takes around 10 to 12 weeks for them to grow strong enough to leave the nest. Even then, they stick close to their parents for a while, learning how to hunt and survive on their own.

Bald Eagles and Flight

One of the most breathtaking things about bald eagles is the way they fly. Unlike smaller birds that flap their wings quickly, bald eagles are built for soaring. They spread their wings wide and ride the air currents, hardly flapping at all. This helps them conserve energy, allowing them to travel long distances without getting tired.

Bald eagles can reach speeds of up to 40 miles per hour while gliding. When diving to catch prey, they can reach speeds of **100 miles per hour**. Their strong wings and hollow bones help them stay light while still being powerful. Their tails act like rudders, helping them steer as they move through the sky.

Because of their flight skills, bald eagles can travel hundreds of miles in search of food. Some even migrate during certain times of the year, moving to warmer areas when lakes and rivers freeze over. Other bald eagles stay in one place year-round, especially in regions where food is always available.

The Sound of a Bald Eagle

Even though bald eagles look fierce, they don't sound as intimidating as you might think. In movies and TV shows, they are often given the call of a red-tailed hawk—a loud, piercing scream. But their actual call is quite different. Bald eagles make high-pitched whistles and chirps that don't match their powerful appearance. Their calls are more like quick, sharp notes rather than deep, booming cries.

They use their voices to communicate with their mates, warn other eagles to stay out of their territory, and call out to their young. While their real call isn't as dramatic as the ones you hear in movies, it's still an important way for them to interact with each other.

Bald eagles are more than just impressive hunters or strong fliers. They play a key role in nature, keeping the ecosystem balanced. By controlling fish and small mammal populations, they help maintain a healthy environment. They've been an important symbol for centuries, but they are also an important part of the natural world.

Why is it called a "bald" eagle?

The bald eagle isn't actually bald. That might sound strange, but the name comes from an old English word, **"piebald,"** which means "white-headed." Over time, people dropped the "pie" part, and the name simply became "bald." If you've ever seen an adult bald eagle, the name makes sense. Its bright white head stands out against its dark brown body, making it one of the most recognizable birds in North America.

A young bald eagle, however, looks completely different. When it hatches, it's covered in soft, grayish-white down, like a fluffy blanket. As it grows, those downy feathers are replaced by dark brown ones. Instead of the crisp white head and tail that adults have, young bald eagles are mostly brown with lighter speckles. If you didn't know better, you might not even recognize them as bald eagles. They look more like golden eagles, another large bird of prey found in North America. It takes around five years for a bald eagle to develop its famous white head and tail. Until then, it blends in with its surroundings, which helps keep it safe from predators.

The white feathers on an adult bald eagle serve more than just an aesthetic purpose. They make it easier for eagles to spot each other from a distance. Since bald eagles often live near large bodies of water, they need a way to recognize potential mates, rivals, or intruders quickly. The stark contrast between the white head and dark body helps them stand out in their environment, whether they're soaring high in the sky or perched on a tree.

Another reason the white head is important is for identifying age and maturity. In the eagle world, the white head is a sign of experience. It tells other eagles that this bird is fully grown and ready to establish its own territory. Younger eagles, still in their brown feathers, often avoid challenging adults.

The white head is like a badge that signals strength and dominance. Once an eagle reaches adulthood, it's ready to find a mate and start building a nest, something it will return to year after year.

Fun facts about bald eagles

Bald eagles are full of surprises. They might be best known for their powerful flight and striking white heads, but there's much more to these birds than meets the eye. From their massive nests to their incredible eyesight, bald eagles have some pretty fascinating traits that set them apart from other birds.

Bald eagles build some of the largest nests of any bird species. These nests aren't just big—they're enormous. A typical bald eagle nest is about four to five feet wide and two to four feet deep. That's already huge, but some nests grow even larger. The biggest bald eagle nest ever recorded was **over nine feet wide and twenty feet deep**. It weighed nearly **two tons**—as much as a small car. These birds don't build a new nest every year. Instead, they return to the same one, adding more sticks and branches each season. Over time, a simple nest can turn into a massive structure that dominates the treetops.

Their eyesight is one of the most impressive of any animal. A bald eagle can spot a small fish in the water from **over a mile away.** That's about four to five times better than human vision. Their eyes are specially designed for long-distance sight, with more light receptors and a second eyelid called a **nictitating membrane** that helps keep their vision sharp. This allows them to lock onto their prey from high above, diving at the perfect moment to snatch it out of the water.

Bald eagles don't just fly—they **soar.** Unlike smaller birds that flap their wings constantly, bald eagles use rising air currents, called **thermals,** to stay in the air without much effort. By riding these warm air pockets, they can glide for hours while barely moving their wings. This helps them conserve energy, making it easier to travel long distances. Some bald eagles migrate thousands of miles each year, following food sources as the seasons change. Others stay in one place year-round, as long as they have a steady food supply.

Their grip is one of the strongest in the animal kingdom. A bald eagle's talons can squeeze with **400 pounds of pressure per square inch.** That's about ten times stronger than the grip of an average human hand. Their sharp, curved claws are designed to hold onto slippery fish, but they can also grasp small mammals and birds. Once an eagle locks onto its prey, it's almost impossible to escape. Their feet are covered in rough, spiky pads called **spicules**, which help them keep a firm grip on whatever they catch.

Bald eagles are incredibly loyal. They usually mate for life, forming strong bonds with their partners. A pair of bald eagles will return to the same nesting area year after year, working together to build and maintain their home. During courtship, they perform dramatic aerial displays, locking talons and spinning through the sky. These behaviors help strengthen their bond before settling down to raise their young.

Despite their powerful appearance, bald eagles don't actually make loud, fierce calls. In movies and television, their sounds are often replaced with the scream of a red-tailed hawk. In reality, bald eagles have a much higher-pitched call that sounds more like a series of whistles or chirps. It's a surprisingly soft sound for such a strong bird, but it plays an important role in communication between mates, young eagles, and rivals.

Their feathers are incredibly lightweight, even though they have thousands of them. A bald eagle has around **7,000 feathers** covering its body. These feathers help with insulation, keeping the bird warm in cold temperatures. They also play a role in aerodynamics, allowing the eagle to control its movements in the air. Despite the large number of feathers, they don't add much weight. The total weight of all a bald eagle's feathers is less than a pound, which helps keep them light enough to soar effortlessly.

Bald eagles have a special way of dealing with cold weather. While some migrate to warmer areas, others stay in freezing regions year-round. Their feathers trap heat close to their bodies, and they can fluff them up to create extra insulation. Their feet don't have feathers, but they have a special adaptation that keeps them from freezing. The blood vessels in their legs are arranged in a way that helps regulate temperature, preventing frostbite even in icy conditions.

They are also known for stealing food. While bald eagles are excellent hunters, they sometimes take an easier route and snatch meals from other birds, especially ospreys. If an osprey catches a fish, a bald eagle might chase it down, forcing it to drop its catch. The eagle then swoops in and grabs the fish before it hits the water. This behavior, called

kleptoparasitism, might seem lazy, but it's actually a smart way to conserve energy. Instead of using up valuable energy hunting, the eagle lets another bird do the work and takes advantage of the opportunity.

Despite being powerful hunters, bald eagles sometimes eat things that are already dead. They are opportunistic feeders, meaning they'll take whatever food is available. This includes carrion—animals that have already died. In the wild, scavenging is an important survival strategy. By eating dead animals, bald eagles help clean up the environment, preventing disease from spreading. They play an essential role in maintaining a balanced ecosystem.

Bald eagles can live a long time. In the wild, they typically live **20 to 30 years**, but some have been known to live even longer. The oldest recorded bald eagle in the wild lived to be 38 years old. In captivity, where they don't have to face predators or harsh weather, they can live even longer. Their long lifespan makes them one of the longest-living birds of prey in North America.

These birds have been a symbol of strength and freedom for centuries, but they were once in danger of disappearing. Habitat destruction, hunting, and the use of harmful chemicals like **DDT** caused their population to drop dramatically in the 20th century.

By the 1960s, bald eagles were on the brink of extinction in the United States. Thanks to conservation efforts and legal protections, their numbers have recovered. Today, bald eagles are no longer considered endangered, and their population continues to grow.

2

THE SYMBOL OF A NATION

The bald eagle wasn't always the obvious choice for America's national symbol. In fact, not everyone agreed that it should represent the country. But today, it's hard to imagine the United States without it. From government buildings to money, military emblems to sports teams, the bald eagle is everywhere. It stands for power, independence, and freedom.

When the United States became an independent nation in 1776, leaders needed a national emblem—something that would represent the strength and character of the country. Other countries had their own symbols. England had the lion, a symbol of bravery and power. France had the rooster, which stood for vigilance and strength. The United States needed something just as bold, something that would reflect the ideals of the new nation.

Congress assigned a group of men, including Thomas Jefferson, John Adams, and Benjamin Franklin, to come up with ideas. They suggested different designs, but none of them included a bald eagle. Instead, Franklin wanted a turkey, believing it was a more respectable bird. He thought turkeys were hardworking and uniquely American, while bald eagles, he claimed, were lazy and stole food from other birds. His idea didn't catch on, and most people found the turkey unimpressive.

The bald eagle, on the other hand, was seen as strong, fierce, and noble. It was unique to North America, making it a natural choice for a symbol that represented the new country. Unlike the turkey, which spent most of its time on the ground, the bald eagle soared high above rivers and mountains. It was a skilled hunter, a powerful flyer, and a majestic sight in the wild. The image of a bald eagle stretching its wings wide seemed to fit perfectly with the spirit of freedom and strength that the young United States wanted to represent.

In 1782, the bald eagle was officially chosen to be

the central figure on the **Great Seal of the United States.** The Great Seal is a special emblem used on official government documents and other important items. It features an eagle with its wings spread wide, holding an olive branch in one talon and a bundle of arrows in the other. The olive branch symbolizes peace, while the arrows stand for the country's willingness to defend itself. In its beak, the eagle carries a banner that reads "**E Pluribus Unum,**" a Latin phrase meaning "Out of many, one." This represents the idea that the United States was formed from many different states coming together as one nation.

Once the bald eagle became the official national symbol, it started appearing everywhere. It was added to coins, government buildings, military insignia, and flags. Over time, it became one of the most recognized symbols of the United States. People admired the bald eagle's ability to soar high above the land, strong and free. It represented the very qualities the country wanted to uphold.

Despite its high status as the national bird, the bald eagle faced serious threats in the years that followed. Habitat destruction, hunting, and the use of harmful pesticides nearly wiped them out. By the mid-1900s, their population had dropped to dangerously low numbers. The bird that had once been chosen to symbolize the nation's strength was struggling to survive. Fortunately, conservation efforts helped bring the bald eagle back, and today, it is once again thriving across North America.

The Great Seal of the United States

The bald eagle isn't just a symbol of America—it's the centerpiece of one of the country's most important emblems: **the Great Seal of the United States.** This seal is used on official government documents, passports, military commissions, and treaties. It's a sign that something is coming directly from the U.S. government. But the seal wasn't something that appeared overnight. It took years of debate and design before it was finally approved, and the bald eagle played a major role in that decision.

When the United States declared independence in 1776, its leaders knew they needed an official seal to represent the new country. Other nations had their own seals, often featuring animals, shields, or coats of arms. A seal wasn't just for decoration—it was a sign of authority, showing that a document or agreement was legitimate. Without a seal, official papers didn't carry the same weight.

Congress put together a group to design the seal, which included **Thomas Jefferson, John Adams, and Benjamin Franklin.** They had ideas, but none of them featured a bald eagle. Instead, they focused on historical and mythological figures, such as Moses leading the Israelites or the goddess Liberty. Their designs were detailed, but none were quite right.

Over the next six years, different artists and committees worked on the seal, trying to create a design that truly represented the spirit of the new nation. In 1782, **Charles Thomson**, the secretary of Congress, proposed the final design, which included the bald eagle as the central figure. This time, the choice was clear. The eagle, with its sharp eyes and outstretched wings, symbolized strength, freedom, and independence. Congress approved the design on **June 20, 1782,** making it the official Great Seal of the United States.

The design is packed with symbolism. At the center of the seal is a **bold, powerful bald eagle** with its wings spread wide. It faces to its right, toward an **olive branch** in its talon. The olive branch represents peace, showing that the United States values diplomacy and wants to work with other nations. In its other talon, the eagle holds a bundle of **thirteen arrows,** which stand for the original thirteen colonies and the country's willingness to defend itself if necessary. Together, the olive branch and arrows show that the nation seeks peace but is prepared for war if needed.

The eagle's beak holds a ribbon with the Latin phrase **"E Pluribus Unum"**, which means **"Out of many, one."** This phrase was chosen to reflect the idea that the United States was formed from many individual colonies coming together as a single nation. At the time, this was a powerful message, reminding people that unity was the country's strength.

On the eagle's chest is a **shield with thirteen red and white stripes and a blue top,** representing the original colonies and the strength of the government. The red and white stripes stand for bravery and purity, while the blue represents vigilance and justice. Unlike other parts of the seal, the shield has no support beneath it. This was intentional—it symbolizes that the new nation had to stand on its own, without relying on any other country.

Above the eagle's head, thirteen **stars form a**

constellation, enclosed in a radiant cloud. This part of the design represents the new nation rising among the other powers of the world. The number thirteen is repeated throughout the seal to honor the original thirteen colonies, a reminder of how the country began.

Once the Great Seal was approved, it started appearing on official documents, government buildings, and even the backs of U.S. coins. One of the most well-known places it appears is on the back of the **one-dollar bill**. If you look closely, you'll see two sides of the seal: one with the eagle, and another with an unfinished pyramid topped by an eye, representing strength and lasting endurance.

Other animals that were considered

One of the most well-known alternatives was the **wild turkey**, famously suggested by Benjamin Franklin. He believed the turkey was a better choice than the bald eagle because it was hardworking and truly American. Wild turkeys are native to North America and had been an important source of food for Native American tribes and early settlers. Franklin argued that turkeys were intelligent, resourceful, and showed great courage when defending themselves.

Turkeys are known to be aggressive when threatened. They will puff up their feathers, spread their tails, and make loud gobbling sounds to scare off intruders. Franklin saw this as a sign of bravery. He even went as far as to criticize the bald eagle, calling it a bird of "bad moral character" because it often stole food from other birds instead of hunting for itself.

But while the turkey had its strengths, most people didn't think it was the right symbol for a new nation. For one thing, it was already a common source of food. People associated turkeys with meals, not majesty. Unlike the bald eagle, which soared high in the sky, the turkey spent most of its time on the ground. It didn't have the same bold and powerful image that leaders wanted for the United States.

Another animal that was considered was the **rattlesnake.** This might sound surprising, but at the time of the American Revolution, the rattlesnake was already a symbol of defiance and independence. Colonists had used it on flags and political cartoons as a warning to their enemies. One of the most famous images was a drawing of a rattlesnake cut into pieces, representing the colonies, with the words "Join, or Die" beneath it. Later, the **Gadsden flag**, which showed a coiled rattlesnake with the words "Don't Tread on Me," became another popular symbol of American resistance.

The rattlesnake had qualities that made it a strong candidate. It was unique to North America, just like the bald eagle. It didn't attack unless provoked, but when it did, it was fast and deadly. This was seen as a reflection of the new country's approach to war—it wouldn't strike first, but it would defend itself fiercely.

Despite its symbolism, the rattlesnake had a major problem: its reputation. Most people saw snakes as dangerous and untrustworthy. Unlike a soaring eagle, a rattlesnake stayed low to the ground and didn't have the same visual impact. It might have worked well on flags and political messages, but as the face of a nation, it wasn't quite right.

Some people suggested the **lion**, a traditional symbol of strength and leadership. Many European countries, including England, used lions on their coats of arms and royal emblems. Lions had been symbols of power for centuries, appearing in myths and historical artworks. A lion would have sent a strong message, but it had one major flaw: it wasn't native to North America. The United States wanted a symbol that truly represented the land and the people, and lions had no connection to the country's wildlife.

The **bison**, also called the American buffalo, was another option. Bison were massive, powerful animals that roamed the Great Plains in huge herds. They were important to many Native American tribes, providing food, clothing, and tools. Their strength and endurance made them a natural choice for a national symbol.

Bison were tough animals that could survive harsh conditions, which made them a good representation of the country's resilience. However, they were mostly found in the western territories at the time, while many of the early U.S. leaders lived in the east. The bison didn't have the same universal recognition across the colonies as the bald eagle. It was an important American animal, but it wasn't as visually striking as a bird with outstretched wings.

Some people even suggested the **wolf**. Wolves were known for their intelligence, teamwork, and strong leadership within their packs. They were feared but also respected. Like the rattlesnake, the wolf had appeared in colonial symbols and early American stories.

But just like the rattlesnake, the wolf had an image problem. Many people saw wolves as dangerous predators that attacked livestock and settlements. Instead of representing strength and unity, they were often hunted as threats. This negative reputation made it unlikely that the wolf would ever be chosen as the national symbol.

3

THE BALD EAGLE IN NATIVE AMERICAN CULTURE

Long before the bald eagle became a symbol of the United States, it held deep meaning for many Native American tribes. The eagle was more than just a bird; it was a messenger, a protector, and a powerful connection to the spirit world. Different tribes had their own beliefs and traditions, but across North America, the bald eagle was respected as a sacred and important creature.

Many tribes believed that the bald eagle carried prayers to the heavens. Its ability to soar high above the land, closer to the sky than any other animal, made it a link between humans and the spiritual world. Some saw the eagle as a messenger that delivered thoughts and wishes to the Creator. Because of this, eagle feathers were often used in ceremonies and rituals, helping people communicate with higher powers.

The Lakota, Dakota, and Nakota—who make up the Sioux Nation—considered the bald eagle a symbol of courage, wisdom, and strength. Warriors who showed great bravery in battle were sometimes honored with eagle feathers. These feathers weren't given out lightly. They had to be earned through acts of heroism and were treated with great care. A warrior who received an eagle feather might wear it in his hair or attach it to his clothing as a mark of honor. If a person received multiple feathers, they could be woven into a headdress, a powerful symbol of leadership and respect.

The Cherokee also saw the bald eagle as a special and sacred bird. They believed that eagles had a direct connection to the thunder beings, powerful spirits associated with storms and weather. Because of this, eagle feathers were used in healing rituals and ceremonies meant to bring balance to nature. The feathers weren't just decorations—they carried deep spiritual meaning and were handled with great respect.

For the Hopi people, the eagle was tied to prayers for rain and a good harvest. They believed the eagle had a special relationship with the natural world, and by honoring it, they could bring blessings to their land. During certain ceremonies, Hopi men would wear headdresses and dance to represent the eagle, showing their respect for the bird's power and grace.

The Haudenosaunee, also known as the Iroquois Confederacy, placed the bald eagle at the top of their Great Tree of Peace. They believed that the eagle's sharp vision allowed it to watch over the people, keeping an eye out for danger. If threats approached, the eagle would warn them, protecting their way of life. This idea reflected the role of leaders within the confederacy, who were expected to be wise, watchful, and protective of their people.

Eagle feathers were often used in sacred objects, such as prayer fans and staffs, which were passed down through generations. These items were not treated as simple decorations—they were sacred and had to be cared for properly. Some tribes held ceremonies when collecting eagle feathers, thanking the bird for its gift and ensuring that the feathers were used with respect.

The bald eagle's ability to fly high and see far made it a symbol of vision and wisdom. Many tribes saw the eagle's keen eyesight as a lesson for humans, reminding them to look at the bigger picture and think carefully before making decisions. The idea that a leader should "see like an eagle" meant being aware of not just what was happening in the moment, but also what was coming in the future.

How feathers were used in ceremonies and traditions

Eagle feathers have long been considered sacred in Native American cultures. They weren't just ordinary feathers—they carried deep spiritual significance and were used in many important ceremonies and traditions. Because the bald eagle was seen as a messenger between humans and the Creator, its feathers were believed to hold great power. They were given as marks of honor, used in prayers, and played a role in rituals that brought people together.

Receiving an eagle feather was one of the highest honors a person could achieve. It wasn't something that could be bought or taken casually. Feathers had to be earned through acts of bravery, wisdom, or service to the community. Warriors who showed exceptional courage in battle might receive an eagle feather to recognize their bravery. Leaders who made wise decisions or helped their people in times of need could also be given feathers as a sign of respect. The process of awarding a feather was often accompanied by a special ceremony, where the recipient was reminded of their responsibilities to their people.

The Lakota and other Plains tribes held **"wiping of the tears"** ceremonies, where eagle feathers were used to help those who had lost loved ones. The feather represented a connection to the spirit world, offering comfort and strength to those in mourning. By placing a feather in their hands or brushing it over them, tribal elders helped people heal from grief and feel supported by their ancestors.

In many tribes, eagle feathers were an important part of headdresses. The more feathers a person had, the greater their achievements. A single feather could be worn in the hair or attached to clothing, while multiple feathers could be woven into elaborate headdresses. These weren't just decorations—they told a story of a person's life and accomplishments. Each feather had meaning, representing an important moment or action that had contributed to the well-being of the tribe.

Feathers were also used in **prayer fans**, which were made by attaching multiple feathers to a handle. These fans were used during ceremonies to carry prayers upward, just as an eagle flies high into the sky. Some fans were simple, while others were decorated with beads, leather, or other materials to make them more personal. During certain rituals, people would wave the fans while singing or chanting, believing that the movement helped their prayers reach the Creator.

During healing ceremonies, eagle feathers were used to bless individuals who were sick or in need of guidance. Medicine people or spiritual leaders would pass the feather over a person's body, believing that it could help remove negative energy and bring balance. This was part of a larger belief that everything in nature was connected, and the eagle's ability to soar high above the land made it a link between the physical and spiritual worlds.

Certain tribes had special **"Feather Dances"**, where eagle feathers were carried or worn as part of a performance. These dances weren't just for entertainment—they were acts of gratitude, meant to honor the eagle and the gifts it provided. The movements of the dancers often imitated the way eagles flew, showing respect for the bird's grace and power.

Stories and myths about the bald eagle

Among the Lakota and other Plains tribes, the eagle was often seen as a messenger between humans and the Great Spirit. Because it could fly higher than any other bird, it was believed to carry prayers to the heavens. Some stories described the eagle as a guardian that watched over the people, offering protection and guidance. Its sharp eyes were said to see not only the land below but also into the future, making it a symbol of wisdom and foresight.

The Hopi people told stories of the eagle's role in bringing rain. They believed the eagle had a connection to the clouds and could influence the weather. During certain ceremonies, eagle feathers were used in prayer rituals to call for rain, ensuring that crops would grow and the land would remain fertile. The eagle was honored as a sacred being that worked in harmony with the earth, the wind, and the sky.

Among the Haudenosaunee (Iroquois), the eagle was a key part of their Great Tree of Peace legend. In this story, the Haudenosaunee Confederacy—made up of five (later six) tribes—was formed to bring peace among warring nations. The tree symbolized unity and strength, and at the very top sat an eagle, watching for danger. It was said that if the eagle ever spotted a threat, it would cry out to warn the people below. This story reinforced the idea that leaders should be like eagles, always looking ahead and protecting those they serve.

In the Pacific Northwest, the eagle was seen as a link between the land and the sky. Some tribes believed that eagles had the power to communicate with the spirits of their ancestors. Their feathers were often used in ceremonies to honor the dead, ensuring that their spirits would find peace and remain connected to the living. The eagle's ability to soar above the mountains and rivers made it a symbol of freedom, strength, and endurance.

Some tribes told stories about the eagle's generosity. They believed that when the eagle shed its feathers, it was offering a gift to the people. Feathers were never taken lightly—they were received with gratitude and used with great care in ceremonies and rituals. It was a reminder that the eagle was not only a hunter and a warrior but also a giver of wisdom and protection.

4

BALD EAGLES IN THE WILD

Bald eagles are found only in North America, making them one of the most iconic birds on the continent. They live in many different places, from the dense forests of Canada to the warm coastal regions of Florida. No matter where they are, they have one thing in common—they always stay close to water. Lakes, rivers, and coastlines provide a reliable source of food, and bald eagles depend on fish for much of their diet.

Alaska has the largest population of bald eagles in the world. The state's rugged wilderness and cold climate might seem harsh, but bald eagles thrive there. With thousands of lakes and rivers teeming with salmon, Alaska provides the perfect hunting grounds. Some areas have such an abundance of fish that bald eagles gather in large numbers, often perching on tree branches near the water, waiting for the right moment to swoop down and grab their next meal.

While Alaska is home to more bald eagles than anywhere else, they are also common in the Pacific Northwest, the Great Lakes region, and parts of the Southeastern United States. In these areas, they nest in tall trees near large bodies of water. Some bald eagles even live in urban areas, as long as they can find food and a place to nest. They have been spotted near cities, flying over bridges, and even nesting on cell towers or tall buildings when natural nesting sites are limited.

Bald eagles are known for building some of the largest nests of any bird species. These nests, called **aeries**, are often placed high up in trees, sometimes over 100 feet above the ground. Eagles choose trees that are strong enough to support their massive nests and tall enough to provide a clear view of the surrounding area. Having a high nest keeps eggs and young eaglets safe from predators while also giving the adult eagles a good vantage point to spot food.

Building a bald eagle nest takes time and effort. Both the male and female work together, bringing sticks, moss, and grass to shape their home. They weave the sticks together, making sure the nest is sturdy. As the nesting season goes on, they add softer materials, such as feathers and dried leaves, to make the inside more comfortable for their eggs.

A newly built eagle nest is already impressive, usually measuring **four to six feet wide** and **two to four feet deep.** However, bald eagles reuse the same nest year after year, adding new materials each season. This means their nests can grow to massive sizes over time. Some nests have reached **over nine feet wide and twenty feet deep**, weighing more than a thousand pounds. One of the largest recorded bald eagle nests was found in Florida and weighed nearly **two tons.**

Because bald eagles are territorial, they don't build their nests close to other eagles. They prefer to have a large area to themselves, which helps them secure a steady food supply. If a pair of bald eagles returns to the same nest each year, they will defend it from other birds, ensuring that it remains their home for as long as possible.

Once the nest is complete, the female lays **one to three eggs**, which both parents take turns keeping warm. It takes about **35 days** for the eggs to hatch, and when the eaglets emerge, they are completely helpless. At first, they rely entirely on their parents for food and protection. The adults bring them fish, tearing off small pieces to feed them. Over time, the eaglets grow stronger, stretching their wings and practicing flapping before they are ready to take their first flight.

What they eat and how they hunt

Bald eagles are powerful hunters with sharp talons, excellent vision, and a strong beak. They are **carnivores**, which means they eat meat, and their favorite food is fish. Living near water gives them plenty of opportunities to find their next meal. Whether they are swooping down to catch a fish from a lake or stealing food from another bird, bald eagles have several ways to get what they need to survive.

Fish make up most of a bald eagle's diet. They prefer species that swim close to the surface, such as **salmon, trout, and catfish**. Their eyesight is so sharp that they can spot a fish from **over a mile away**. Once they see one, they dive toward the water, extending their massive talons at just the right moment. Their claws pierce the fish's slippery scales, and their strong grip keeps it from escaping. Once the fish is secure, the eagle flaps its wings hard to lift back into the air. If the fish is too heavy, the eagle may struggle to carry it and could even be pulled under. In these cases, some eagles have been known to **paddle to shore using their wings like oars**, refusing to let go of their catch.

While fish are their favorite, bald eagles eat a variety of other animals. They sometimes hunt **small mammals** like **rabbits, squirrels, and muskrats**. If the opportunity presents itself, they will also take **waterfowl**, such as ducks and geese. Hunting birds is more difficult than catching fish because birds are fast and unpredictable. However, bald eagles are patient hunters. They will wait for the right moment to strike, using their speed and precision to grab their prey in midair.

Unlike some hunters that only eat what they catch, bald eagles **scavenge** when necessary. They don't mind eating an animal that has already died, such as a deer carcass or a fish that washed up on shore. In colder months, when hunting can be more challenging, they rely on scavenging more often. This may seem like an easy way to get food, but it actually helps keep the environment clean by removing dead animals that could spread disease.

Stealing food is another tactic bald eagles use to get a meal. They often take food from smaller birds, especially **ospreys**, which are expert fish hunters. If an osprey catches a fish, a bald eagle might chase it through the sky, forcing it to drop its catch. Once the fish falls, the eagle swoops in and grabs it before it hits the water. This behavior, called **kleptoparasitism**, might seem unfair, but it's a smart way to conserve energy. By letting another bird do the hard work, the eagle can get a meal without using as much effort.

Bald eagles are **opportunistic feeders**, meaning they take advantage of whatever food is available. While they prefer fresh meat, they will eat almost anything they can catch or find. This flexibility helps them survive in different environments, from remote wilderness areas to places where human activity has changed the landscape.

Once they catch their food, bald eagles use their sharp, curved beaks to tear it into pieces. They don't chew their food like mammals do. Instead, they swallow large chunks, breaking them down in their stomachs. Their digestive systems are designed to handle bones, fur, and scales, so they can eat nearly every part of their prey. Whatever they can't digest gets compacted into a small pellet and spit out later.

The role of bald eagles in the ecosystem

Bald eagles may be powerful hunters, but they do more than just catch fish and soar through the skies. They play an important role in the ecosystem, helping to keep the environment balanced. As top predators, they control populations of fish and small animals. As scavengers, they clean up dead animals that could spread disease. Their presence in the wild is a sign of a healthy environment, and when bald eagles thrive, it often means the entire ecosystem is in good shape.

One of the most important jobs bald eagles have is keeping fish populations in check. Because fish make up the largest part of their diet, eagles help control the number of fish in lakes, rivers, and coastal waters. They often target weaker or slower fish, which prevents overcrowding and helps maintain a balanced ecosystem. If too many fish live in one area, food sources can run low, affecting the health of the entire population. By hunting, bald eagles help make sure fish populations stay stable, creating a healthier environment for all species that rely on those waters.

Bald eagles also help regulate populations of small mammals and birds. While fish are their main food source, they sometimes hunt rabbits, squirrels, ducks, and even smaller birds. Without predators like eagles, some animals could multiply too quickly, leading to overpopulation. If a certain species grows too large in numbers, it can throw the ecosystem out of balance by using up too many resources. Predators like bald eagles play a key role in making sure this doesn't happen.

In addition to hunting, bald eagles are scavengers. They often feed on dead animals, such as fish that have washed up on shore or animals that have died from natural causes. This helps clean up the environment, preventing disease from spreading. Without scavengers like eagles, decaying animals would take much longer to break down, leading to the spread of bacteria and attracting pests. By eating carrion, bald eagles act as nature's cleanup crew, keeping their habitat healthier for all species.

Their nests also have an impact on the environment. Because bald eagles return to the same nests year after year, their massive structures provide shelter for other animals. When an eagle nest is abandoned or falls apart, smaller birds and mammals sometimes move in, using the leftover materials to build their own homes. This creates opportunities for different species to thrive, showing how eagles contribute to the ecosystem even when they're not around.

Another way bald eagles influence the ecosystem is through their presence as an **indicator species.** This means that scientists can study bald eagle populations to understand the health of an environment. Because eagles sit at the top of the food chain, they are affected by changes in their habitat. If their numbers start to decline, it can be a warning sign that something is wrong, such as pollution or habitat destruction. When bald eagles are doing well, it usually means that the water is clean, the fish populations are healthy, and the overall ecosystem is balanced.

5

ALMOST GONE

For thousands of years, bald eagles soared through the skies of North America, thriving in forests, near lakes, and along coastlines. They were powerful hunters, expert fishers, and symbols of strength. But by the 20th century, something was terribly wrong. Their numbers were dropping fast. In places where bald eagles had once been common, they were disappearing. By the 1960s, they were on the brink of extinction in the United States.

Many people didn't realize at first what was happening. Bald eagles had been a strong and resilient species for centuries, so their decline seemed sudden. But it wasn't caused by just one problem—it was a combination of several threats, all happening at the same time.

One of the biggest reasons for their decline was **hunting**. In the 1800s and early 1900s, people viewed bald eagles very differently than they do today. Instead of seeing them as majestic birds, many saw them as pests. Farmers and ranchers believed bald eagles were a threat to their livestock, especially young lambs and chickens. Even though eagles mostly hunted fish and small animals, people assumed they would attack farm animals as well. Because of this, bald eagles were shot and killed in large numbers.

Hunting wasn't just limited to farmers. Some people shot bald eagles for sport, and others hunted them to sell their feathers. At one point, a government program even encouraged the killing of bald eagles in Alaska, offering **bounties**—money paid to people who killed them. Thousands of bald eagles were lost because of these misunderstandings and fears.

Another major problem was **habitat destruction**. As the human population grew, cities and towns expanded into areas where bald eagles once nested. Large forests were cut down for lumber, and wetlands were drained to make space for roads and buildings. Since bald eagles rely on tall trees near water to build their nests, this destruction made it harder for them to find safe places to raise their young. With fewer nesting sites, their population continued to shrink.

Pollution also played a role. As industries grew, chemicals and waste were dumped into lakes and rivers. This poisoned the water and reduced the number of fish bald eagles depended on for food. If there wasn't enough food, fewer eagle chicks survived, making it even harder for the population to recover.

But the biggest threat of all came from **DDT**, a chemical pesticide that was widely used after World War II. DDT was sprayed on crops to kill insects and stop the spread of diseases like malaria. It seemed like a helpful invention, but people didn't realize how much damage it was causing to wildlife.

When DDT entered the environment, it didn't just stay on plants. Rain washed it into rivers and lakes, where fish absorbed it. Bald eagles, who ate the fish, unknowingly took in large amounts of DDT. The chemical didn't kill the eagles directly, but it **weakened their eggshells**. Instead of being strong and protective, eagle eggs became thin and fragile. When the mother eagle sat on them to keep them warm, they cracked under her weight. This meant fewer and fewer baby eagles were hatching.

As more eggs failed, bald eagle populations dropped to dangerously low levels. By the 1960s, they had nearly disappeared from the lower 48 states. In some places, they were completely gone. A bird that had once symbolized the strength of a nation was now on the edge of extinction.

The impact of pollution, hunting, and habitat destruction

Bald eagles had ruled the skies of North America for thousands of years, but by the mid-1900s, their numbers were shrinking fast. The threats weren't coming from natural predators or food shortages. Instead, they were facing dangers created by people. Pollution, hunting, and habitat destruction had combined to create a crisis that pushed them toward extinction.

Each of these problems affected bald eagles in different ways. Some made it harder for them to find food. Others took away the safe places they needed to build their nests. Some even weakened their eggs, preventing new generations from hatching. The damage built up over time, and before anyone realized what was happening, bald eagles were disappearing from places where they had once been common.

The Damage of Pollution

Pollution was one of the biggest threats to bald eagles, and it came in many forms. Some types of pollution poisoned their food, while others ruined the places they lived.

Factories and farms dumped chemicals into rivers and lakes, which were the same waters where bald eagles hunted for fish. These chemicals didn't just stay in the water. Small fish absorbed them, and when larger fish ate the smaller ones, the chemicals built up in their bodies. By the time a bald eagle caught one of these fish, the poison had become strong enough to affect the eagle itself.

One of the worst pollutants was **DDT**, a pesticide used to kill insects. It was sprayed on crops and entered the water supply, making its way into fish and, eventually, into bald eagles. DDT didn't kill adult eagles directly, but it caused **eggshell thinning**. When an eagle laid eggs, the shells were so fragile that they cracked under the weight of the mother keeping them warm. Without strong eggs, fewer baby eagles were hatching, and the population continued to drop.

Oil spills also became a major problem. When oil tankers spilled into the ocean, the slick spread across the water, coating everything in its path. Fish and birds struggled to survive in the toxic mess. Bald eagles that hunted in these areas swallowed poisoned fish or got oil on their feathers, making it difficult for them to fly and stay warm.

Even the air was affected. As factories burned coal and released pollutants, **acid rain** formed and fell over forests and lakes, damaging ecosystems. It made the water more acidic, which killed fish and other wildlife. With fewer fish to eat, bald eagles struggled to find enough food to survive.

The Toll of Hunting

Bald eagles were once seen as a threat rather than a treasure. Farmers and ranchers believed that they attacked livestock, especially young lambs and chickens. While bald eagles rarely went after farm animals, the belief was strong enough that many people shot them on sight. Some states even encouraged the killing of bald eagles by offering **bounties**, paying hunters for each eagle they killed.

In Alaska, more than **100,000 bald eagles** were killed under a bounty system that lasted for decades.

Hunters were not just farmers protecting their animals—some people killed eagles for sport, while others did it for their feathers, which were sold illegally. The government later recognized that these killings were based on misinformation, but by then, the damage had already been done.

Poisoning was another form of hunting that hurt bald eagles. Some farmers placed **poisoned bait** in fields to kill wolves, coyotes, or other predators. Bald eagles, scavengers by nature, often ate these poisoned animals and became sick themselves. Lead poisoning was also a problem. Hunters used lead bullets, and when eagles ate the remains of hunted animals, they accidentally consumed the lead, which poisoned their bodies over time.

Losing Their Homes

As cities grew, forests and wetlands shrank. Bald eagles needed tall trees near water to build their nests, but as more land was cleared for buildings, roads, and farms, the number of suitable nesting sites declined. Without a safe place to lay their eggs, many eagles couldn't raise their young successfully.

Logging also played a role. When large trees were cut down for wood, it didn't just affect the forests—it took away the very trees that bald eagles relied on for survival. Without these strong, high trees, eagles were forced to nest in weaker, less stable locations, which put their eggs at risk.

Dams built on rivers changed the way water flowed, disrupting fish populations. Since bald eagles depended on fish, these changes made it harder for them to find food. Fewer fish meant fewer meals, and some bald eagles had to abandon their nests and search for food elsewhere, often with little success.

How DDT nearly wiped them out

Bald eagles had survived for thousands of years, adapting to changes in their environment and continuing to thrive. But by the mid-1900s, something strange was happening. Their numbers were plummeting, and no one could figure out why. Eagles were still finding food, and they weren't being hunted as much as before. Yet their population was dropping at an alarming rate. Scientists soon discovered the cause—a chemical called **DDT**.

DDT was first used in the 1940s as a **pesticide**, a chemical designed to kill insects that damaged crops or spread diseases like malaria. It was sprayed on farms, forests, and even in neighborhoods to get rid of mosquitoes and other pests. At first, people saw

DDT as a miracle chemical. It was cheap, effective, and easy to use. Farmers relied on it to protect their crops, and cities used it to keep insects under control.

What people didn't realize was that DDT wasn't just killing insects. It was **spreading through the environment** and affecting wildlife in ways no one had expected. Rain washed DDT into lakes and rivers, where it was absorbed by **tiny organisms called plankton**. Small fish ate the plankton, and larger fish ate the small fish. Each time the chemical moved up the food chain, it became more concentrated. By the time bald eagles ate the contaminated fish, they were getting a dangerously high dose of DDT.

At first, the eagles seemed fine. They weren't getting sick or dying immediately. But something was wrong with their eggs. Female eagles were laying eggs as usual, but instead of being strong and protective, the **eggshells were too thin and fragile.** When mother eagles sat on their eggs to keep them warm, the shells cracked under their weight. The eggs couldn't survive, which meant fewer and fewer baby eagles were hatching.

This problem, known as **eggshell thinning**, was devastating. Bald eagles are slow to reproduce. A pair of eagles usually lays only **one to three eggs per year**, and not every egg hatches successfully. With so many eggs failing to hatch, entire generations of eagles were being lost.

The impact was massive. In the early 1900s, there had been **hundreds of thousands** of bald eagles in North America. By the 1960s, there were only about **400 nesting pairs left in the lower 48 states**. The bird that had once been a symbol of strength and freedom was disappearing.

Scientists and conservationists became alarmed. They knew something had to be done before bald eagles vanished completely. Researchers studied the effects of DDT on birds, collecting eggs from nests and testing their thickness. The evidence was clear—DDT was weakening the eggs, and if nothing changed, bald eagles could go extinct.

Public awareness grew, and people began to demand action. In **1972**, the United States banned DDT, marking a turning point in the fight to save bald eagles. It was a major victory for conservation, but the damage had already been done. Bald eagle populations were still dangerously low, and it would take years for them to recover.

The ban on DDT was just the first step in bringing bald eagles back. Scientists and environmentalists worked together to protect nesting sites, restore habitats, and breed eagles in captivity to help increase their numbers. Slowly, their population began to rise. The chemical that had nearly wiped them out was finally out of their system, and with time, bald eagles started hatching successfully again.

6

SAVING THE BALD EAGLE

By the time bald eagles were declared an endangered species in the United States, their population had dropped to dangerously low levels. The chemical **DDT** had weakened their eggs, hunting had wiped out thousands of them, and habitat destruction had left them struggling to find safe places to nest. For a species that had once been so powerful, their survival was now hanging by a thread.

Scientists, conservationists, and lawmakers realized something had to be done. If people had caused the problem, then people had to be the ones to fix it. The bald eagle wouldn't recover on its own—laws and protections had to be put in place to give the species a chance to survive.

One of the first major laws designed to protect bald eagles was the **Bald Eagle Protection Act of 1940**. This law made it illegal to hunt, kill, sell, or own bald eagles, including their feathers, eggs, and nests. Before this law, bald eagles were often shot by hunters, ranchers, and farmers who mistakenly believed the birds were a threat to livestock. The law was a big step forward, but it wasn't enough. At the time, people still didn't realize how much of a threat DDT and habitat destruction were to the species. Even though hunting bald eagles was now illegal, their numbers continued to drop.

By the 1960s, it was clear that stronger protections were needed. The **Endangered Species Act of 1973** became one of the most important laws in American history for protecting wildlife. It provided funding for conservation programs and gave the government the power to protect animals on the verge of extinction. The bald eagle was placed on the **endangered species list**, which meant its habitat, nests, and food sources were now protected by law.

Another crucial step was the **ban on DDT** in 1972. The government recognized the damage DDT was doing to birds, especially bald eagles, and decided to outlaw its use in the United States. Once

DDT was removed from the environment, eagles began laying stronger eggs, and more eaglets started hatching.

The **Migratory Bird Treaty Act** also played a role in protecting bald eagles. Originally created in 1918 to protect birds that migrate between countries, this law made it illegal to disturb or harm bald eagles and their nests. Anyone caught taking an eagle's feathers, eggs, or disturbing a nest could face heavy fines or even jail time.

To help rebuild the bald eagle population, scientists launched **breeding and reintroduction programs**. Eggs were carefully monitored to ensure they were hatching properly. Baby eagles were raised in protected environments before being released into the wild. In areas where bald eagles had disappeared completely, young eagles were introduced to help reestablish populations.

Conservation groups and wildlife agencies also worked to **restore habitats** by protecting forests, wetlands, and other key nesting areas. Bald eagles need tall trees near water to build their nests, and as more land was set aside for conservation, they began to return to areas where they had once disappeared.

How scientists and conservationists helped

After decades of decline, bald eagles were in serious trouble. Laws like the **Bald Eagle Protection Act** and the **Endangered Species Act** had been passed to prevent people from hunting and disturbing them, but laws alone weren't enough. The damage had already been done. Eagles were still struggling with habitat loss, food shortages, and the lingering effects of **DDT**. Simply making it illegal to harm them wasn't going to bring them back. They needed direct help.

Scientists and conservationists stepped in with one goal—to save the bald eagle before it disappeared forever. Their work involved researching eagle populations, restoring habitats, monitoring nests, and even **raising young eagles in captivity** to release them into the wild.

One of the first steps scientists took was **tracking bald eagle populations** to find out exactly how many were left. By the 1960s, bald eagles had disappeared from many parts of the country. Some states had fewer than five nesting pairs, and in some areas, there were none at all. Researchers began **surveying nests**, counting eggs, and monitoring which ones actually hatched. What they found was alarming. Even in nests where eagles were laying eggs, very few were surviving. Many cracked before the chicks could hatch, and those that did hatch were often too weak to survive.

The biggest problem was **DDT**, which had caused eagle eggshells to thin. When this was discovered, scientists worked to collect as much evidence as possible to prove that DDT was harming not just bald eagles, but many other birds as well. Their research played a major role in getting **DDT banned in 1972**. That was a huge step, but bald eagles still needed help to recover.

Conservationists turned their attention to **habitat restoration**. Eagles need tall trees near lakes and rivers to build their nests, but deforestation had destroyed many of these areas. To fix this, conservation groups worked to protect forests and wetlands, ensuring that eagles had safe places to nest and hunt. Some organizations bought land specifically to set aside as eagle sanctuaries, making sure the birds had undisturbed places to raise their young.

Scientists also launched **captive breeding programs** to help boost the bald eagle population. In these programs, eagles were raised in controlled environments, where their eggs were carefully monitored to prevent breakage. When young eagles were strong enough to survive on their own, they were released into the wild. This process, known as **hacking**, had been successfully used with other endangered birds and became a key strategy for bald eagle recovery.

Hacking involved placing young eagles in artificial nests, often on tall platforms in areas where bald eagles had disappeared. Conservationists would feed them without being seen, ensuring that the birds didn't become dependent on humans. Once the eaglets were old enough to fly, they left the nesting site and began living in the wild on their own. Over time, hacked eagles adapted to their new homes, mated, and began rebuilding the population.

Another major effort involved **nest protection programs**. Scientists and volunteers monitored bald eagle nests to make sure eggs and chicks weren't disturbed. If a nest was in danger—whether from human activity, predators, or storms—teams stepped in to help. Some eggs were carefully relocated to safer areas, while others were placed in incubators until they were ready to hatch.

To prevent bald eagles from being poisoned by

lead, conservationists worked to educate hunters about switching to **non-lead ammunition**. Lead bullets left behind in animal carcasses were a major source of poisoning for eagles that scavenged for food. Wildlife groups spread awareness about the dangers of lead, and over time, many hunters began using safer alternatives.

Bald eagles today

Bald eagles have made an incredible comeback. After nearly disappearing from the United States, their numbers have grown, and they can now be seen soaring through the skies in many parts of the country. Laws, conservation efforts, and habitat protection played a big role in their recovery. Because of these efforts, the bald eagle was officially removed from the **endangered species list in 2007**. That was a huge success, but it doesn't mean they are completely safe. While they are no longer at risk of extinction, new challenges continue to threaten their survival.

One of the biggest dangers bald eagles still face today is **habitat loss**. Even though conservationists have worked to protect nesting areas, human development continues to expand into eagle territory. Forests are cleared for new buildings, roads, and farmland, which means fewer tall trees for eagles to nest in. Since bald eagles return to the same nesting sites year after year, losing a nesting tree can force them to relocate or prevent them from raising young.

Pollution remains another serious problem. Although **DDT** is no longer used in the United States, other chemicals still make their way into lakes and rivers. Mercury and other heavy metals build up in fish, which can harm bald eagles when they eat contaminated prey. Plastic pollution is also a growing issue. Eagles sometimes mistake plastic for food or get tangled in discarded fishing lines and nets. These threats are harder to control than hunting or habitat destruction because they come from many different sources.

One of the most unexpected dangers bald eagles now face is **collisions with human-made structures.** Power lines, wind turbines, and vehicles have all become common hazards. Eagles fly long distances in search of food and often don't see power lines until it's too late. Some conservation groups have worked with power companies to install protective coverings on power lines to prevent electrocution, but accidents still happen.

Wind energy is another challenge. While wind turbines provide clean energy, they can also be dangerous to large birds like bald eagles. Eagles often hunt by soaring over open areas, which is exactly where wind farms are built. Efforts are being made to reduce the number of bird collisions, but it remains a concern for conservationists.

Lead poisoning is still a major issue. Even though many hunters have switched to non-lead ammunition, lead bullets and fishing tackle are still used in some areas. When eagles scavenge on carcasses left behind by hunters, they can ingest tiny fragments of lead, which poisons their bodies over time. Conservationists continue to educate hunters about using safer alternatives, but lead exposure remains a serious threat to bald eagle health.

Climate change is another factor that may impact bald eagles in the future. Rising temperatures can affect fish populations, making food harder to find in certain areas. Changing weather patterns also impact nesting success. If storms become more frequent or severe, they could destroy nests or make it harder for eaglets to survive.

Even though bald eagles have recovered,

continued conservation efforts are needed to keep their population stable. Many wildlife organizations still monitor eagle nests, track population numbers, and work to protect important habitats. Laws like the **Bald and Golden Eagle Protection Act** remain in place to prevent harm to the species.

7

BALD EAGLES AND AMERICAN PRIDE

Bald eagles have made a strong comeback, and today, they can be found soaring over rivers, perched on tall trees, and nesting along coastlines across the United States. While they were once on the brink of extinction, conservation efforts have helped their population grow, and now, people have a much better chance of spotting these incredible birds in the wild. They are still most common in areas with large bodies of water, where fish are plentiful, but they have also expanded into unexpected places.

One of the best places to see bald eagles is **Alaska.** The state has the highest bald eagle population in the country, with more than **30,000** of them living there. They are often spotted near rivers, especially during the salmon runs when fish are abundant. One of the most famous spots is **Haines, Alaska,** where thousands of bald eagles gather along the Chilkat River each fall. This gathering, known as the **Alaska Bald Eagle Festival,** draws birdwatchers from around the world who come to witness the eagles hunting and interacting with each other.

The **Pacific Northwest** is another stronghold for bald eagles. Washington and Oregon both have large eagle populations, particularly near the **Puget Sound** and along the **Columbia River.** These areas provide a mix of forests and waterways, making them ideal habitats for nesting and hunting. In Washington, the **Skagit River Bald Eagle Natural Area** is a well-known wintering spot where eagles gather in large numbers to feed on salmon.

The **Mississippi River** is one of the best places in the **Midwest** to see bald eagles, especially during the winter. As lakes and smaller rivers freeze, eagles flock to the open waters of the Mississippi, where they can still find fish. Cities like **Dubuque, Iowa,** and **Alton, Illinois,** have special viewing areas where visitors can watch eagles diving for fish or perching on ice-covered branches. The **National Eagle Center in Wabasha, Minnesota,** is dedicated to educating people about bald eagles and even has live eagles that cannot be released into the wild.

In the **Northeastern United States,** bald eagles have rebounded in states like **New York, Pennsylvania, and Maine.** One of the best places to see them is **Conowingo Dam in Maryland,** where eagles gather to catch fish near the dam's rushing waters. The **Hudson River Valley** in New York is another popular location, especially during the winter months.

The **Southeastern U.S.** has also seen a rise in bald eagle populations. **Florida** has one of the largest concentrations of bald eagles outside of Alaska. The state's warm climate and abundance of lakes make it a perfect year-round home for these birds. The **Everglades,** the **Merritt Island National Wildlife Refuge,** and the **Kissimmee River** are all great places to see bald eagles in flight.

Even in places where bald eagles were once completely gone, they are now returning. States like **Texas, Tennessee, and Georgia** have seen eagle populations grow in recent years. In some areas, nests have been found near cities, showing that bald eagles can adapt to different environments as long as they have food and safe places to raise their young.

How bald eagles are still used as symbols

One of the most well-known places the bald eagle appears is in **government symbols**. The **Great Seal of the United States** features a bald eagle at its center, holding an olive branch in one talon and a bundle of arrows in the other. This seal is used on official documents, passports, and even military badges. The eagle represents the country's commitment to peace, symbolized by the olive branch, while also showing strength and readiness to defend itself with the arrows. The bald eagle also appears on the **Presidential Seal**, a symbol used by the President of the United States.

Bald eagles are seen across **the U.S. military**, representing courage and power. The **United States Marine Corps** uses an eagle in its emblem, perched on a globe with an anchor behind it. The **101st Airborne Division**, one of the most famous military units, is nicknamed the **"Screaming Eagles"**, and its patch features a bald eagle's head. The bird is also found on several military medals, including the **Medal of Honor**, the highest award given to U.S. soldiers for bravery in combat.

In **sports**, bald eagles are a popular choice for team mascots and logos. Many professional and college teams use the eagle's fierce image to represent strength, speed, and determination. One of the most well-known teams is the **Philadelphia Eagles**, an NFL football team that has used an eagle in its logo since the 1930s. The team's mascot, **Swoop**, is a bald eagle, and their fans proudly wave flags featuring the bird's image.

Many college teams also use bald eagles as their mascot, including the **Boston College Eagles**, the **Eastern Washington Eagles**, and the **Auburn Tigers**, whose battle cry is "War Eagle." These teams chose the bald eagle because it represents dominance and leadership, qualities they want their athletes to embody on the field.

Outside of sports, bald eagles can be found in **business logos** and branding. Many American companies use the bird's image to suggest strength, reliability, and patriotism. The eagle is often used in the logos of banks, car companies, and airlines. **American Eagle Outfitters**, a popular clothing brand, uses an eagle as its logo to represent freedom and adventure. Even **the U.S. Postal Service** has used the bald eagle in its logo, symbolizing swift and dependable service.

Bald eagles also appear on **U.S. currency**. The back of the **quarter** features a bald eagle in some designs, and the bird has been used on coins and dollar bills throughout history. The eagle's presence on money reinforces its status as a national icon, representing economic strength and stability.

What kids can do to help protect bald eagles and other wildlife

Bald eagles have made an incredible comeback, but their survival depends on people continuing to protect them. Many of the problems that once pushed bald eagles to the edge of extinction—pollution, habitat loss, and illegal hunting—haven't completely disappeared. While scientists and conservationists work hard to keep bald eagle populations strong, protecting wildlife is something everyone can take part in. Even kids can make a difference.

One of the simplest ways to help bald eagles and other animals is by **keeping the environment clean**. Trash and pollution don't just make places look messy—they can harm wildlife in serious ways. Plastic bags, fishing lines, and other litter can get caught in an eagle's talons or around its beak, making it difficult for the bird to hunt or eat. Small pieces of plastic can be swallowed by fish, which are then eaten by eagles, spreading harmful chemicals through the food chain. Picking up trash in parks, on hiking trails, or near rivers can help keep these areas safe for wildlife.

Recycling is another way to make a positive impact. When people recycle plastic, paper, and metal, it reduces the amount of garbage that ends up in landfills and natural habitats. Many animals, including bald eagles, are affected by pollution from landfills, especially when toxic materials seep into water sources. By recycling and reducing waste, kids can help keep nature clean and safe for all species.

Protecting **trees and green spaces** is also important. Bald eagles rely on tall trees near water to build their nests, but as forests are cleared for buildings and roads, their nesting sites disappear. Planting trees in backyards, schoolyards, or parks can provide birds with shelter and safe places to rest. Supporting efforts to protect forests and wetlands helps ensure that bald eagles and other wildlife have homes for years to come.

Another way to help is by **learning about wildlife and sharing that knowledge with others.** Understanding how bald eagles live, what they eat, and what threatens their survival helps people see why conservation matters. Kids can talk to their family and friends about the importance of protecting wildlife, write about bald eagles for school projects, or create posters and presentations to spread awareness. The more people know about wildlife conservation, the more likely they are to help.

Wildlife-friendly choices at home can also make a difference. Using **non-toxic household products** helps prevent chemicals from getting into rivers and lakes where bald eagles hunt. Avoiding pesticides in gardens and choosing eco-friendly products reduces pollution in the environment. Even small changes, like turning off lights to save energy or using reusable water bottles instead of plastic ones, contribute to a healthier planet.

Supporting organizations that protect bald eagles is another great way to help. Many wildlife groups work to rescue injured eagles, protect their nesting sites, and educate people about conservation. Some organizations even allow people to "adopt" a bald eagle by donating money to help care for the birds. These programs support important efforts like habitat restoration and research to keep eagle populations strong.

8

AMAZING BALD EAGLE FACTS
THE BIGGEST BALD EAGLE NESTS

Bald eagles are known for building some of the **largest nests of any bird in the world.** Unlike many birds that start fresh every year, bald eagles return to the same nest, adding new materials each season. Over time, these nests can grow to **huge** sizes, weighing hundreds—or even thousands—of pounds.

One of the biggest bald eagle nests ever found was discovered in **St. Petersburg, Florida.** It measured **9.5 feet wide, 20 feet deep, and weighed nearly 3 tons (6,000 pounds).** That's about as heavy as a small car. The nest was built in a large tree and was used by the same pair of eagles for many years.

Another massive nest was found in **Ohio,**

measuring **8.5 feet wide and 12 feet deep**. Scientists believe the same eagles had been adding to it for more than 30 years. Since bald eagles mate for life and use the same nest each year, some nests become towering structures that look more like giant tree forts than bird homes.

Building and maintaining a nest this large requires serious dedication. Eagles use **sticks, moss, grass, and feathers** to make sure their home is both sturdy and comfortable. Some nests are passed down from one generation to the next, allowing them to grow larger over time.

The Longest Bald Eagle Flights

Bald eagles are strong fliers and can cover **huge distances** in search of food. While they usually stay within a certain range near their nest, some eagles have traveled thousands of miles across North America.

One of the longest recorded bald eagle migrations was tracked using a GPS tracker attached to a young eagle. The bird flew over **2,000 miles** from Canada to the southern United States, crossing rivers, mountains, and forests along the way. Some eagles that breed in **Alaska** travel south to **California or even Mexico** for the winter, following food sources as the seasons change.

Bald eagles can also reach **impressive speeds** while flying. When gliding, they move at about **30 to 40 miles per hour**, but when diving, they can reach speeds of **over 100 miles per hour**. Their powerful wings allow them to soar for hours without flapping, riding wind currents to save energy.

The Oldest Bald Eagles

In the wild, bald eagles typically live between **20 and 30 years**, but some have lived much longer. The oldest known bald eagle in the wild was tracked through a **banding program**, where scientists placed a small metal band on its leg to study its movements. This eagle was at least **38 years old** when it was found in **New York**.

Eagles in captivity can live even longer because they don't face predators, food shortages, or harsh weather. Some have lived to be **50 years old** or more. One of the oldest captive bald eagles was an eagle named **"Freedom"**, who lived in a wildlife sanctuary for over **50 years** after being rescued from an injury.

The fact that bald eagles can live for decades means they play an important role in their environment for a long time. A single pair of eagles can raise dozens of chicks over their lifetime, helping to keep the population strong.

Bald eagle superpowers

Super Vision: How Bald Eagles See the World

One of the most powerful tools a bald eagle has is its **vision**. If humans had the eyesight of an eagle, they would be able to see an ant crawling on the ground from the top of a ten-story building. Scientists estimate that an eagle's vision is at least **four to five times sharper than a human's.**

Eagles have something called **binocular vision**, which means both of their eyes work together to focus on one object at a time. This helps them judge distances incredibly well, which is important when swooping down to catch fast-moving prey. Their eyes also have more **light-sensitive cells** than human eyes, allowing them to spot small movements from high above the ground.

Another special feature of eagle eyesight is their ability to see **more colors than humans.** They can detect **ultraviolet light,** which helps them track prey in ways people can't even imagine. For example, some animals leave behind trails of urine that reflect ultraviolet light, making it easier for eagles to track them. This gives them an extra advantage when hunting on land.

Eagles also have a **third eyelid,** called a **nictitating membrane.** This thin, clear layer slides across the eye from side to side, acting like a built-in pair of goggles. It protects their eyes from dust, water, and bright sunlight while still allowing them to see.

Incredible Speed: How Fast Can a Bald Eagle Fly?

Bald eagles aren't just great at seeing their prey —they're also incredibly fast when they go in for the catch. While gliding through the air, eagles usually fly at speeds of around **30 to 40 miles per hour.** But when they're hunting, they can reach speeds of up to **100 miles per hour** in a steep dive.

Their **powerful wings,** which can stretch up to **seven feet wide,** allow them to soar for long periods without flapping. By riding on rising warm air currents, called **thermals,** eagles can glide thousands of feet into the sky, using very little energy. From these great heights, they scan the ground and water below, waiting for the perfect moment to strike.

Even though eagles are large birds, their **hollow bones** make them surprisingly lightweight. Their bones are strong but filled with air pockets, which helps them stay in the sky with less effort. This is why they can soar for hours, barely moving their wings, and only flapping when they need to pick up speed.

Super Strength: How Powerful Is an Eagle's Grip?

One of the most shocking facts about bald eagles is the strength of their **talons.** Their grip is so powerful that they can **crush bones** and hold onto fish that weigh more than they do.

The strength of an eagle's grip comes from **sharp, curved talons** and incredibly strong leg muscles. Their talons can generate a force of **400 pounds per square inch (PSI).** To put that into perspective, a human's hand grip is around **20 to 40 PSI.** That means an eagle's grip is **ten times stronger** than the average person's.

Once an eagle locks its talons around something, it's nearly impossible for the prey to escape. The tendons in their feet have a special **ratcheting mechanism** that allows them to **lock** their grip without using extra muscle strength. This helps them carry heavy prey for long distances without tiring out their legs.

Even though bald eagles mainly eat fish, their talons are strong enough to grab **ducks, rabbits, and**

even small deer. If the prey struggles, the eagle tightens its grip, digging its sharp claws deeper. Some eagles have been known to **drag fish out of the water that weigh up to 15 pounds,** almost twice the weight of the eagle itself.

Fun trivia

Surprising Bald Eagle Facts

- **They don't sound like you think they do.** In movies and TV shows, bald eagles are often given the call of a red-tailed hawk—a loud, piercing scream. But their real call is much softer, more like a high-pitched whistle or chirp. It's not quite as fierce as their appearance might suggest.
- **They can swim.** If a bald eagle catches a fish that's too heavy to carry, it won't always let go. Instead, it might use its wings to **paddle** to shore, dragging the fish along with it. Their wings work like oars, helping them move through the water.
- **They don't get their white heads right away.** When bald eagles hatch, they are

covered in grayish-brown down feathers. It takes **about five years** for them to develop the white head and tail feathers that make them so recognizable. Until then, they look more like golden eagles.

- **Their nests can weigh more than a car.** Some bald eagle nests grow to be **as heavy as 6,000 pounds**. That's about the weight of a small car or a grand piano. These giant nests are made up of sticks, moss, and grass and are built up year after year.

- **They have a special way of holding onto prey.** Their talons lock in place once they grab something, meaning they don't have to use muscle power to hold on. This is useful when carrying heavy fish or prey over long distances.

- **They can fly higher than most birds.** Bald eagles can soar as high as **10,000 feet** in the air. That's nearly two miles above the ground! They use rising warm air currents, called thermals, to lift themselves higher with little effort.

- **Their eyes are bigger than a human's.** Even though a bald eagle's head is much smaller than a person's, its eyes are about the same size. This helps them see incredible details from far away, making them some of the best hunters in the sky.

www.ingramcontent.com/pod-product-compliance
Ingram Content Group UK Ltd.
Pitfield, Milton Keynes, MK11 3LW, UK
UKHW031506250225
455528UK00008B/88

9 798348 503826